COFAs To

Related titles from Law Society Publishing:

Anti-Bribery Toolkit
Amy Bell

COLPs Toolkit
Michelle Garlick

Outcomes-Focused Regulation
Andrew Hopper QC and Gregory Treverton-Jones QC

The Solicitor's Handbook 2012
Andrew Hopper QC and Gregory Treverton-Jones QC

All books from Law Society Publishing can be ordered through good bookshops or direct from our distributors, Prolog, by telephone 0870 850 1422 or e-mail **lawsociety@prolog.uk.com**. Please confirm the price before ordering.

For further information or a catalogue, please contact our editorial and marketing office by e-mail **publishing@lawsociety.org.uk**.

COFAs Toolkit

Jeremy Black and Florence Perret du Cray

The Law Society

ISBN 978-1-907698-47-7

Published in 2012 by the Law Society
113 Chancery Lane, London WC2A 1PL

Reprinted in 2012 (twice)

Typeset by Columns Design XML Ltd, Reading
Printed by TJ International Ltd, Padstow, Cornwall

The paper used for the text pages of this book is FSC® certified. FSC (the Forest Stewardship Council®) is an international network to promote responsible management of the world's forests.

Contents

About the authors

Jeremy Black

Jeremy Black is a partner in Deloitte's Professional Practices industry team where he has worked for 17 years. He spends most of his time advising professional practice clients including large and mid-size UK and international law firms.

Jeremy provides firms with advice on a variety of financial matters including compliance with the client money regulations. He has assisted firms in a number of operational areas including financing, working capital management and the use of key performance indicators. In addition Jeremy has provided strategic input to firms' merger discussions as well as performing due diligence work on both domestic and international mergers.

Jeremy holds an MBA in legal practice and in 2002, as part of the qualification, he wrote a research project on the implications of outside ownership of law firms. Jeremy has been at the forefront of Deloitte's Legal Services Act initiatives and he has worked with a number of firms in connection with the alternative business structure regime and its implications for the provision of legal services in the UK.

Florence Perret du Cray

Florence Perret du Cray joined Deloitte in 2002. She worked in the firm's Professional Practices group for a number of years where she was involved in the audit of law firms. In 2005 she moved to Deloitte's National Audit and Accounting department where she provides technical advice to audit engagement teams and works on the firm's compliance with regulatory requirements.

About Deloitte

Deloitte provides professional services to a range of clients across the UK and Europe, including audit, consulting, corporate finance, risk management and tax services. Deloitte LLP is the United Kingdom member firm of Deloitte Touche Tohmatsu Limited (DTTL), a UK private company limited by guarantee, whose member firms are legally separate and independent entities. For more information about Deloitte visit **www.deloitte.co.uk**.

Foreword

While it is fair to say that many firms have been identifying and managing risks for a long time, the demands of the Legal Services Act 2007 and the introduction of outcomes-focused regulation (OFR) by the Solicitors Regulation Authority (SRA) mean that all firms – whatever their shape, size or location – must prioritise risk management.

Instead of adhering to a precise set of rules the profession is now working toward a list of outcomes, supported by indicative behaviours, and this change in approach brings with it a greater focus on regulating the practice as well as the individual solicitor.

To help firms meet their legal and regulatory obligations, the Law Society established its Risk and Compliance Service a little over a year and a half ago. To date, the Service's compliance support includes bespoke in-house consultancy, webinars, monthly e-newsletters, master classes, seminars and conferences.

It is important for solicitors to be aware that they will not need to re-work all their systems and procedures in the light of the SRA Code of Conduct 2011. This is particularly pertinent for sole practitioners, who are often the senior partner, law firm manager and risk professional rolled into one.

With these things in mind, the Law Society's Risk and Compliance Service in collaboration with a number of subject matter experts has commissioned this series of hands-on toolkits.

These practical guides have been prepared with the busy practitioner in mind. They aim to help reduce the cost of compliance for practitioners by providing a useful set of reference notes, definitions, best practice tips and templates. Much of their content is informed by first-hand information gleaned through onsite risk diagnostic visits and interactions with members of the profession, and in response to practitioner requests for tools to assist in their compliance journey.

Our hope is that these toolkits rapidly become 'must-have' elements in every practitioner's compliance armoury and to this end I recommend them to you without reservation.

The Risk and Compliance Service would like to thank Jeremy Black and Florence Perret du Cray for their contribution to the creation of the *COFAs Toolkit*.

Pearl Moses
Risk and Compliance Manager
The Law Society

Preface

On 6 October 2011, the SRA introduced OFR. In a move away from the previous rules-based approach, this new regulatory framework focuses on high-level outcomes governing the management of authorised bodies and the quality of outcomes for clients.

The new regulations require that each practice must now appoint a compliance officer for legal practice (COLP) to ensure compliance with regulatory requirements and a compliance officer for finance and administration (COFA) to ensure, along with other responsibilities, compliance with the SRA Accounts Rules.

The COFA has a significant role to play in assisting the practice in its compliance with the new regulations and, as such, it is essential for the nominated individuals to fully understand the nature of the obligations imposed and when those obligations commence.

This toolkit has been designed to provide practical assistance to COFAs and to enable them to discharge their responsibilities effectively. It highlights the principal regulatory requirements relevant to COFAs, explains their role and responsibilities and contains useful guidance as well as a range of practical tools. The documents contained in the toolkit should be tailored to suit the particular needs and circumstances of the individual practices.

This toolkit is based on the law and SRA regulatory requirements as at 23 April 2012. At the time of going to press, the SRA have stated that a web-based nomination form for COLPs and COFAs will be available from **www.sra.org.uk** from 31 May 2012 with nominations to be submitted by 31 July 2012.

We hope that you will find this toolkit useful both as a reference guide and as a practical resource in your day-to-day work.

We would like to thank Andrew Lowes and Philippa Hutton for their contribution.

Jeremy Black and Florence Perret du Cray
Deloitte
April 2012

1 Overview of the principal regulatory requirements relevant to COFAs

The SRA has published a handbook (the SRA Handbook), which brings together in one place, for the first time, all the regulatory requirements that apply to everyone regulated by the SRA.

Figure 1.1 and sections **1.1** to **1.5** provide an overview of the key sections of the SRA Handbook relevant to COFAs.

1.1 The Principles

The SRA Handbook sets out 10 mandatory principles which apply to everyone that the SRA regulates and to all aspects of practice. They are the key ethical requirements for firms and individuals who are involved in the provision of legal services. They stand alone at the beginning of the SRA Handbook and underpin all of the regulatory requirements.

Principles 1 to 6 are similar to the core duties in the Solicitors' Code of Conduct 2007 (2007 Code). Principles 7 to 10 are new and relate to the management of the

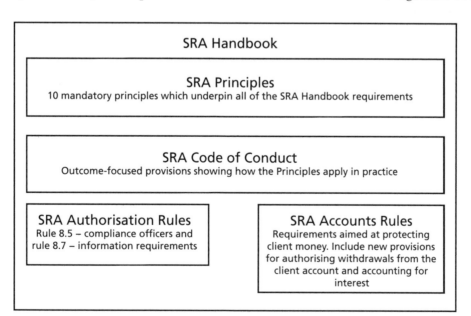

Figure 1.1 Key sections of the SRA Handbook relevant to COFAs

practice and compliance with regulatory arrangements. These new principles reflect the SRA's increased emphasis on business management.

The 10 Principles are:

You must:

1. uphold the rule of law and the proper administration of justice;
2. act with integrity;
3. not allow your independence to be compromised;
4. act in the best interests of each client;
5. provide a proper standard of service to your clients;
6. behave in a way that maintains the trust the public places in you and in the provision of legal services;
7. comply with your legal and regulatory obligations and deal with your regulators and ombudsmen in an open, timely and co-operative manner;
8. run your business or carry out your role in the business effectively and in accordance with proper governance and sound financial and risk management principles;
9. run your business or carry out your role in the business in a way that encourages equality of opportunity and respect for diversity; and
10. protect client money and assets.

Practices are expected to act in accordance with the Principles in everything they do and whenever a COFA has to consider a regulatory issue, their first point of reference should always be the Principles.

1.2 The new Code of Conduct

The SRA Code of Conduct 2011 (2011 Code) is very different from the 2007 Code. Rather than containing prescriptive rules, supported by guidance, it comprises mandatory outcomes and non-mandatory indicative behaviours which may be useful to COFAs in interpreting the SRA regulations.

The different chapters in the 2011 Code set out the outcomes which describe what practices are expected to achieve in order to comply with the Principles in specific contexts.

The indicative behaviours provide examples of the kinds of behaviours which may establish whether practices have achieved the relevant outcomes and complied with the Principles. They are not an exhaustive list of how to comply and, depending upon the circumstances, it is envisaged that it will be possible to achieve outcomes in other ways.

1.3 The SRA Authorisation Rules

The SRA Authorisation Rules for Legal Services Bodies and Licensable Bodies 2011 (SRA Authorisation Rules) set out the requirements that persons or practices must meet to become and remain an SRA authorised person or body. The most relevant rules for COFAs are:

- rule 8.5 (Compliance officers) – requirement for practices to appoint a COFA and the COFA's main responsibilities;
- rule 8.7 (Information requirements) – requirement to report to the SRA.

1.4 The SRA Accounts Rules

The principal purpose of the SRA Accounts Rules 2011 (SRA Accounts Rules) is to protect client money. Large parts of the previous rules have been retained and overall the rules remain very specific and detailed in order to provide a high degree of protection to clients. However, some operational flexibility has been introduced, for example in relation to the payment of interest and signing on client account. These are areas where firms are now able to exercise appropriate judgment without an unnecessary degree of prescription.

1.5 Overseas practice

Specific references to overseas practice are made throughout the SRA Handbook. The Law Society has issued a practice note that lists all the provisions related to overseas practice in one place and sets out any changes in the provisions related to overseas practice from those that pertained under the 2007 Code (see **www. lawsociety.org.uk/productsandservices/practicenotes/overseaspractice.page**). It summarises the main requirements related to overseas practice as follows:

- The Principles – the Principles apply to solicitors or managers of authorised bodies who are practising from an office outside the UK. They also apply if you are a lawyer-controlled body practising from an office outside the UK.
- The Code of Conduct – the 2011 Code applies to solicitors, managers of authorised bodies and lawyer-controlled bodies who practise from an office outside the UK. The provisions relevant to overseas practices are outlined at the end of each chapter of the 2011 Code. One of the key changes from the 2007 Code is in Chapter 7 'Management of your business' (previously dealt with in the 2007 Code under rule 15.05). The new outcomes in Chapter 7, which all apply to overseas practice, now cover:
  - governance;
  - systems and controls to ensure compliance with regulatory requirements;
  - risk assessment and management;
  - systems and controls to monitor financial stability; and
  - supervision, quality assurance and outsourcing.

- The SRA Accounts Rules – Part 7 (rules 47–52) deals with overseas practices.
- The SRA Authorisation Rules – this section of the practice note principally refers to the Law Society practice note on compliance officers.

2 Becoming a COFA

2.1 Who can be a COFA

A COFA must be an individual who is a manager or an employee (as defined in the SRA Handbook Glossary) of the authorised body, who has been designated as its COFA and whose designation has been approved by the SRA. An individual must consent to designation as a COFA and not be disqualified from acting as a head of finance and administration (HOFA) as defined by the Legal Services Act 2007. Unlike the COLP, an individual appointed to the role of COFA does not have to be a lawyer.

As a significant part of the COFA's role relates to the SRA Accounts Rules it is important that the COFA has a good understanding of the rules as well as a general understanding of financial matters.

The guidance to the SRA Authorisation Rules states that the practice should ensure that individuals appointed to the roles of COLP and COFA should be of sufficient seniority and in a position of sufficient power and responsibility to fulfil their role (guidance note (vi) to rule 8 of the SRA Authorisation Rules). There is no definition of what sufficient seniority or in a position of sufficient responsibility might mean but note (vi) explains that compliance officers should have 'clear reporting lines to enable them to have access to all management systems and arrangements and all other relevant information including client files and business information'.

The roles of COLP and COFA can be carried out by the same person, provided that they have the necessary skills to fulfil both roles.

Practices where there may be no one person who currently meets all of these requirements will need to consider updating the practice's systems, governance and reporting lines to allow the COFA to be empowered and to operate as required.

> **Note:** As the role of COFA is new, it may not have been considered at the time the individual to be appointed as COFA negotiated their original employment contract. Practices may consider drafting additional terms of appointment to formalise clear reporting lines, to empower the individual to fulfil their role as COFA, even potentially against the wishes of the managers of the practice, and to document the individual's consent to the role. Illustrative wording and points to consider are provided in **Appendix B**.

2.2 Suitability criteria

This toolkit focuses on the role and responsibilities of the COFA and does not address the SRA's criteria for approval of an individual to the role of COFA. Such criteria are set out in the SRA Suitability Test 2011 in the Authorisation and Practising Requirements section of the SRA Handbook.

2.3 Nomination process

Practices will be able to nominate COLPs and COFAs from 31 May 2012 until 31 July 2012 and approval will be given by the SRA by 31 December 2012. COLPs and COFAs will start fulfilling their duties on 1 January 2013.

To nominate its COLP and COFA, the practice will complete a web-based nomination form that sets out the obligations of the practice under rules 8.1, 8.2 and 8.5 of the SRA Authorisation Rules and the responsibilities of the COLP and COFA under rules 8.5(c) and (e). It is based on binding declarations by both a manager with authority to sign on behalf of the practice and the COLP or COFA nominee.

The practice's side of the declaration, signed by a manager, includes confirmation that:

- the practice has suitable arrangements in place to ensure that the COLP or COFA is able to discharge their duties; and
- the COLP's or COFA's declarations, including that the nominee has sufficient seniority and responsibility in the practice, are correct.

The COLP or COFA nominee declares that:

- they understand their obligations and have sufficient responsibility in the practice and are in a position of sufficient seniority to perform the role;
- they are satisfied that the practice's managers have put in place suitable arrangements to ensure that they are able to discharge the COLP or COFA duties in accordance with the rules;
- they will take all reasonable steps to ensure compliance; and
- they consent to being designated as the COLP or COFA.

The nomination form also includes relevant declarations for the SRA Suitability Test (see **2.2** above).

> **Note:** This section on the nomination process is based on the information published on the SRA website at the time of going to press. The SRA has indicated that it will contact all firms and provide further advice and information including obligations placed on those completing the forms. For up-to-date guidance on the registration process and the information to be provided to the SRA, refer to the SRA website: **www.sra.org.uk**.

3 Responsibilities of the COFA

This section addresses the various responsibilities of the COFA as set out in the SRA Handbook. While some of these responsibilities are clearly defined and attributed to the COFA, or are of a financial nature and therefore the COFA may be expected to take ownership of them, others are much broader and apply equally to the COFA and the COLP or the wider practice. For the purposes of this toolkit, these are being referred to as 'primary' and 'secondary' responsibilities. A comparison of the respective responsibilities of the COLP and the COFA is available in the SRA's quick guide to OFR, 'Outcomes-focused regulation at a glance' (at **www.sra.org.uk/solicitors/freedom-in-practice/OFR/ofr-quick-guide.page**).

3.1 Primary responsibilities of the COFA

Rule 8.5(e) of the SRA Authorisation Rules sets out the following primary responsibilities of the COFA:

- take all reasonable steps to ensure that the authorised body and its employees and managers comply with any obligations imposed upon them under the SRA Accounts Rules and record any failure so to comply and make such records available to the SRA on request; and
- as soon as reasonably practicable, report to the SRA any failure to comply.

In order to discharge their primary responsibilities fully, guidance note (ix) to rule 8 of the SRA Authorisation Rules says that COFAs will need to consider whether they are in a position to, for example:

(a) ensure that they have access to all accounting records;
(b) carry out regular checks on the accounting systems;
(c) carry out file and ledger reviews;
(d) ensure that the reporting accountant has prompt access to all the information needed to complete the accountant's report;
(e) take steps to ensure that breaches of the SRA Accounts Rules are remedied promptly;
(f) monitor, review and manage risks to compliance with the SRA Accounts Rules;

Whilst responsibility for day-to-day supervision may be delegated to one or more individuals to enable effective control to be exercised, delegation of total responsibility to a cashier or bookkeeper is not acceptable.

The SRA's quick guide 'Outcomes-focused regulation at a glance' also implies that there is a role for COFAs in reporting when the practice is in serious financial difficulties. COFAs may therefore also need to consider whether they are able to access information on the practice's overall financial status and be in a position to make an assessment of that status and report to the SRA when the practice is in serious financial difficulties.

> **Notes:** Terms of appointment to the role of COFA agreed between the individual and the practice, as referred to in **2.1**, may assist COFAs when considering whether they are in a position to discharge their role fully.
>
> The 'SRA guidelines – accounting procedures and systems' checklist included as **Appendix D** is designed to assist the COFA when monitoring compliance with the SRA's guidelines on dealings with client money and the SRA Accounts Rules. Adherence to the guidelines, however, does not obviate the need to comply fully with the SRA Accounts Rules. It is therefore recommended that as well as completing and reviewing this checklist on a regular basis, practices also consider maintaining a full list of the SRA Accounts Rules, showing how each individual rule has been addressed.
>
> The following additional templates will assist COFAs in discharging their responsibilities in relation to performing matter file reviews, recording and reporting breaches:
>
> - **Appendix E** Guidance on matter file reviews
> - **Appendix F** Matter file review template
> - **Appendix G** Proforma templates for the recording of breaches internally
> - **Appendix H** Template letter for reporting material breaches to the SRA
> - **Appendix I** Common areas of breaches of the SRA Accounts Rules
>
> Appendix 3 to the SRA Accounts Rules requires practices to determine a policy for dealing with mixed payments. As this is an area where breaches are commonly identified, an example of such a policy has been included at **Appendix J**.

3.2 Secondary responsibilities of the COFA

Chapter 7 of the 2011 Code and rule 8 of the SRA Authorisation Rules make it clear that, whilst overall responsibility rests with the practice and its managers, the compliance officers have a role to play in the efficient running and the regulatory compliance of the practice.

These secondary responsibilities mainly relate to ensuring that the practice has systems and controls in place to enable the practice, as well as its managers, employees and anyone who owns any interest in the practice, to comply with the requirements on them.

In the guidance notes to rule 8 of the SRA Authorisation Rules, the SRA highlights that practices should have suitable arrangements (a 'compliance plan') for compliance with the SRA regulatory requirements and that what needs to be covered by the compliance plan will depend on factors such as the size and nature of the practice, its work and its areas of risk. COFAs should therefore consider whether the following systems and processes suggested by the SRA have been implemented (guidance note (iii) to rule 8):

(a) clearly defined governance arrangements providing a transparent framework for responsibilities within the firm;
(b) appropriate accounting procedures;
(c) a system for ensuring that only the appropriate people authorise payments from client account;
(d) a system for ensuring that undertakings are given only when intended, and compliance with them is monitored and enforced;
(e) appropriate checks on new staff or contractors;
(f) a system for ensuring that basic regulatory deadlines are not missed e.g. submission of the firm's accountant's report, arranging indemnity cover, renewal of practising certificates and registrations, renewal of all lawyers' licences to practise and provision of regulatory information;
(g) a system for monitoring, reviewing and managing risks;
(h) ensuring that issues of conduct are given appropriate weight in decisions the firm takes, whether on client matters or firm-based issues such as funding;
(i) file reviews;
(j) appropriate systems for supporting the development and training of staff;
(k) obtaining the necessary approvals of managers, owners and COLP/COFA;
(l) arrangements to ensure that any duties to clients and others are fully met even when staff are absent.

In addition, the SRA Handbook places numerous reporting requirements on practices, those working within practices and authorised individuals. Many of the requirements apply to the practice as an authorised body. Practices should decide who, within the practice, will make these reports with contingency plans for when nominated individuals are absent. Although in many cases, practices may decide that the person best placed to make these reports is the COLP, the COLP and COFA should liaise closely to ensure that reports are made promptly and that there is no duplication.

To ensure that compliance with the SRA Accounts Rules is enshrined within the firm, systems, policies and procedures will need to be implemented, reviewed, monitored for compliance and improved upon where necessary.

COFAs should keep a record of the systems, policies and procedures put in place and the monitoring performed. It is important to remember that the COFA will not be personally liable for breaches per se, but could be liable for failing to implement, or failing to demonstrate that they have implemented, systems to endeavour to achieve compliance. Whilst it is not mandatory that written records are kept of such systems, policies and procedures, COFAs must ask themselves whether and how they will be able to show that they have suitable arrangements in place to ensure compliance if such records are not kept.

> **Notes:** The 'Overall compliance checklist' available in **Appendix A** lists the reporting requirements that practices are most likely to allocate to the COFA. A complete list of these reporting requirements with references to where the full requirements can be found in the SRA Handbook is available on the Law Society's website at **www.lawsociety.org.uk/new/documents/practicesupport/ reportingrequirements.pdf.**
>
> **Appendix K** provides a framework to assist COFAs in considering whether adequate systems and controls are in place to enable the practice, as well as its managers and employees, to comply with the requirements on them.
>
> **Appendix L** provides examples of key general controls that would be expected to be in place within the practice.

3.3 Reporting breaches

COLPs and COFAs must report to the SRA any failure by the practice to comply with the SRA regulatory requirements and make records available to the SRA on request. Although practices may remedy breaches immediately upon discovery, this does not remove the need for the compliance officers to make a report to the SRA in accordance with the SRA Authorisation Rules where appropriate.

Breaches that are 'material' must be reported to the SRA as soon as reasonably practicable. The immediacy of the report will depend on the circumstances and seriousness of the breach. Non-material breaches will be reported to the SRA as part of the annual information report required under rule 8.7 of the SRA Authorisation Rules.

When determining whether a breach, or a series of breaches, is material, guidance note (x) to rule 8 suggests the COFA will need to consider:

(a)   the detriment, or risk of detriment, to clients;
(b)   the extent of any risk of loss of confidence in the firm or in the provision of legal services;
(c)   the scale of the issue;
(d)   the overall impact on the firm, its clients and third parties.

It is important to note that whilst a single breach may be trivial, if it is part of a series of breaches then it may be material. For this reason, a compliance officer will need systems to identify patterns of breaches.

3.4 Maintaining records

It is a requirement that COLPs and COFAs keep records of all breaches in compliance. Practices may consider putting in place centralised reporting systems to enable them to:

- capture and record all breaches in compliance;
- monitor overall compliance with obligations;
- assess the effectiveness of the practice's systems and put in place measures to mitigate against the risk of further non-compliance;
- comply with the duty to report breaches which are material because they form a pattern.

It will be easier to identify patterns of non-compliance in smaller practices where there are likely to be fewer breaches reported. However, in larger practices there may need to be some system of categorisation of breaches, e.g. by rule breached or area of law, to allow the COLP or COFA to identify patterns of breaches that may need to be reported to the SRA.

> **Note:** A template for the recording of breaches, the identification of patterns of non-compliance and the documentation of remedial actions is provided at **Appendix G.**

3.5 Potential liability of the COFA

As explained above, the responsibilities placed on COFAs are broad. COFAs are responsible for ensuring that the practice has systems and controls in place to enable the practice, its managers and employees to comply with the SRA requirements on them. While the SRA has highlighted that responsibility for compliance ultimately rests with the managers of a practice, compliance officers could also find regulatory action taken against them where they fail to meet their responsibilities.

It is therefore important for COFAs to ensure they are in a position to carry out their role effectively. Even though compliance ultimately rests with the managers of a practice, there may be situations when COFAs report issues to the SRA against the wishes of the managers of the practice. As such, COFAs will need to ensure that they have the authority to do this.

COFAs may feel that without some protection, they will not wish to 'consent' and may wish to consider including indemnity provisions for such circumstances. Director and Officer (D and O) insurance cover may also be available and COFAs and the firm should discuss availability of such cover with brokers. Firms will also want to protect themselves and ensure that they do not have to provide indemnity when a COFA has knowingly been reckless or careless.

> Some suggested wording for indemnity provisions and authorities from the firm to be included in terms of appointment has been provided in **Appendix B**.

3.6 The role of compliance officers in smaller practices

The same responsibilities apply to COLPs and COFAs irrespective of the size of practice. However, smaller practices may face practical problems in identifying an individual of sufficient seniority and responsibility who is also in a position to record all failures to comply with the SRA Accounts Rules.

The SRA has emphasised that what needs to be covered by a practice's compliance plan will depend on factors such as the size and nature of the practice, its work and its areas of risk. Systems and processes should be proportionate to the risks faced by the practice to avoid overly complex systems that are bypassed and therefore become ineffective in practice.

3.7 Contingency planning (absence of the COFA)

Practices should consider how they will manage the absence of the COFA. Where the COFA is likely to be absent for a significant length of time they may need to be replaced. Practices should discuss with the SRA whether replacement is an appropriate action for the practice.

If the practice ceases to have a COFA it must immediately, and in any event within seven days:

* notify the SRA;
* designate another manager or employee to replace the COFA; and
* make an application to the SRA for temporary approval of the new COFA.

Refer to the SRA Authorisation Rules, rule 18 'Temporary emergency approvals for compliance officers' for further guidance.

> Some suggested wording for a letter notifying the SRA that the individual designated as COFA is no longer able to fulfil his/her role as such and to request temporary emergency approval of a new COFA has been included in **Appendix C.**

4 Further guidance

Further guidance available online at the time of printing of this toolkit:

SRA website

- SRA Handbook
  www.sra.org.uk/solicitors/handbook/welcome.page

- Outcomes-focused regulation at a glance
  www.sra.org.uk/solicitors/freedom-in-practice/ofr/ofr-quick-guide.page

- Q&As: Compliance officers for legal practice (COLPs) and compliance officers
  for finance and administration (COFAs)
  www.sra.org.uk/solicitors/freedom-in-practice/ofr/colp-cofa-questions-answers.page

Law Society website

- Summary of the SRA Handbook reporting requirements
  www.lawsociety.org.uk/new/documents/practicesupport/reportingrequirements.pdf

- Compliance officer FAQs
  www.lawsociety.org.uk/practicesupport/regulation/complianceofficersfaqs.page

- Law Society's practice notes
    - Outcomes-focused regulation: overview
      www.lawsociety.org.uk/productsandservices/practicenotes/ofroverview.page
    - Compliance officers
      www.lawsociety.org.uk/productsandservices/practicenotes/complianceofficers.page
    - Overseas practice
      www.lawsociety.org.uk/productsandservices/practicenotes/overseaspractice.page

APPENDIX A

Overall compliance checklist for COFAs

This checklist has been designed to assist COFAs in discharging their responsibilities by providing a framework to document how compliance is achieved and monitored.

COFAs will however need to consider the extent to which this checklist needs to be modified as reporting lines and the allocation of responsibilities between the COLP and the COFA will vary across practices.

Requirement	Source	Templates available in the toolkit	Procedure in place	Work performed to ensure procedure is operating effectively	Satisfactory/ Improvement required/No evidence
1 Becoming a COFA					
1.1 A COFA has been formally appointed and appointment has been notified to the SRA	SRA Authorisation Rules, rule 8.5	Appendix B – Terms of appointment to role of COFA		e.g. Copy of the letter retained on records	
1.2 Obtain and file the SRA's approval of the designation of the firm's COFA	SRA Authorisation Rules, rules 8.5 and 8.6(a)		e.g. The SRA's approval received on [date]	e.g. Copy of the SRA's authorisation retained on records	
2 Compliance with the SRA Accounts Rules					
2.1 Policies and systems are in place to ensure that the practice complies fully with the SRA Accounts Rules	SRA Authorisation Rules, rule 8.5(e) SRA Accounts Rules, Appendix 3: SRA guidelines, para. 2.1 (based on Principle 10 'Protect client money and assets')	Appendix D – SRA guidelines – accounting procedures and systems checklist Appendices E–J	e.g. Completion and periodic review of the 'SRA guidelines – accounting procedures and systems checklist' Note: It is recommended that as well as completing and reviewing this checklist on a periodic basis, practices also consider maintaining a full and detailed list of the SRA Accounts Rules showing how each individual requirement has been addressed		

Requirement	Source	Templates available in the toolkit	Procedure in place	Work performed to ensure procedure is operating effectively	Satisfactory/ Improvement required/No evidence
2.2 Procedures are in place to record failures to comply with the SRA Accounts Rules and such records are available to the SRA on request	SRA Authorisation Rules, rule 8.5(e)	Appendix G – the templates for recording breaches include a column to document remedial actions			
2.3 Material failures to comply with the SRA Accounts Rules (whether a standalone breach or as part of a pattern) are reported to the SRA as soon as reasonably practicable	SRA Authorisation Rules, rule 8.5(e)	Appendix H – Template letter for reporting material breaches to the SRA			
2.4 In relation to 2.1 to 2.3 above, are suitable arrangements in place to ensure that the COFA is able to discharge of his/her duties in accordance with the SRA Authorisation Rules? This includes, but is not limited to:	Guidance note (ix) to rule 8 of the SRA Authorisation Rules	Appendix B – Terms of appointment to role of COFA	e.g. Terms of appointment to the role of COFA have been signed by the individual as well as by the practice, thus evidencing the practice's commitment to formalise clear reporting lines and to empower the individual to fulfil his/her role as COFA	e.g. A copy of the signed terms of appointment is retained on record	
• having access to all accounting records		Appendix B – Terms of appointment to role of COFA			
• carrying out regular checks on the accounting systems					

• carrying out file and ledger reviews		Appendix E – Guidance on matter file reviews Appendix F – Matter file review template			
• ensuring that the reporting accountant has prompt access to all the information needed to complete the accountant's report		Appendix B – Terms of appointment to role of COFA			
• taking steps to ensure that breaches of the SRA Accounts Rules are remedied promptly		Appendix G – the templates for recording breaches include a column to document remedial actions			
• having the authority to report all breaches that are material either on their own or as part of a pattern to the SRA		Appendix B – Terms of appointment to role of COFA			
• being able to monitor, review and manage risks to compliance with the SRA Accounts Rules		Appendix B – Terms of appointment to role of COFA			
2.5 Procedures are established for verifying that the systems in place to comply with the SRA Accounts Rules are operating effectively	SRA Accounts Rules, Appendix 3: SRA guidelines, para. 2.1 Law Society practice note: Compliance officers, section 4.2	Appendix D – SRA guidelines – accounting procedures and systems checklist			e.g. The COFA oversees a quarterly matter file review process. Any deficiencies are documented and reported in compliance with the rules. Bank reconciliations are reviewed on a monthly basis

Requirement	Source	Templates available in the toolkit	Procedure in place	Work performed to ensure procedure is operating effectively	Satisfactory/ Improvement required/No evidence
2.6 Report annually to the SRA in the prescribed format by the prescribed date	SRA Authorisation Rules, rule 8.7(a)				
2.7 Consider whether there is a need to put in place additional measures or alter existing systems to mitigate against the risk of further non-compliance, including additional staff training required	Law Society practice note: Compliance officers, section 6.3	Appendix G – the templates for recording breaches include a column to document remedial actions			
3 Monitoring the financial stability of the firm					
3.1 Systems and controls are in place for monitoring the financial stability of the practice	Principle 8 2011 Code, O(7.4), IB(7.2), IB(10.2)		e.g. Budget, expenditures and cash flows are prepared [annually] and reviewed [monthly]		
3.2 As there is a specific requirement to report promptly to the SRA when the practice is in serious financial difficulties, consider whether you are: • able to access information on the practice's overall financial status and make an assessment of that status • empowered to report to the SRA in the event the practice is in serious financial difficulties	Principle 8 2011 Code, O(10.3)	Appendix B – Terms of appointment to role of COFA			

3.3 Consider whether there is any: • reason for concern about the practice's financial stability • indicator of serious financial difficulty, such as inability to pay the professional indemnity (PI) insurance premium, or rent or salaries, or breach of covenants • awareness that the practice may not be financially viable to continue trading as a going concern, for example because of difficult trading conditions, poor cash flow, increasing overheads, loss of managers or employees and/or loss of sources of revenue If yes, determine whether there is a need to report promptly to SRA	Principle 8 2011 Code, O(7.4), O(10.3), IB(10.2)–(10.4)	e.g. Budget, expenditures and cash flows are prepared reviewed [monthly]		
3.4 Systems and controls are in place for monitoring risks to money and assets entrusted to the practice by clients and others	Principle 8 2011 Code, O(7.4)			
4 Risk management and compliance with the SRA regulatory requirements				
4.1 There are clear and effective governance structure and reporting lines	Principle 8 2011 Code, O(7.1)			

Requirement	Source	Templates available in the toolkit	Procedure in place	Work performed to ensure procedure is operating effectively	Satisfactory/ Improvement required/No evidence
4.2 The practice has a compliance plan which includes effective systems and controls to achieve and comply with all the Principles, rules, outcomes and other requirements of the SRA Handbook applicable to the practice. The following systems and processes suggested by the SRA have been implemented: • a system for ensuring that only the appropriate people authorise payments from client account • a system for ensuring that undertakings are given only when intended, and that compliance with them is monitored and enforced • a system for ensuring appropriate checks on new staff or contractors • a system for ensuring that basic regulatory deadlines are not missed, e.g. submission of the firm's accountant's report, arranging indemnity cover, renewal of practising certificates and registrations, renewal of all lawyers' licences to practise and provision of regulatory information	Principle 8 2011 Code, O(7.2) Guidance note (iii) to rule 8 of the SRA Authorisation Rules	Appendix K – Risk management framework Appendix L – Examples of key general controls			

Checklist item		
• a system for monitoring, reviewing and managing risks • ensuring that issues of conduct are given appropriate weight in decisions the firm takes, whether on client matters or firm-based issues such as funding • file reviews • appropriate systems for supporting the development and training of staff • obtaining the necessary approvals of managers, owners and COLP/COFA • arrangements to ensure that any duties to clients and others are fully met even when staff are absent		
4.3 Risks of non-compliance with all the Principles, rules, outcomes and other requirements of the SRA Handbook applicable to the practice are identified, monitored and managed	Principle 8 2011 Code, O(7.3)	Appendix K – Risk management framework
4.4 Consider the need to report promptly to the SRA when serious failure to comply with or achieve the Principles, rules, outcomes and other requirements of the SRA Handbook have been identified	SRA Authorisation Rules, rule 8.5(e)	Appendix H – Template letter for reporting material breaches to the SRA

Requirement	Source	Templates available in the toolkit	Procedure in place	Work performed to ensure procedure is operating effectively	Satisfactory/ Improvement required/No evidence
5 Other reporting requirements					
5.1 Indicate below the individuals nominated by the practice to report promptly to the SRA regarding the following:					
• information required as part of the annual information gathering exercise by the prescribed date	SRA Authorisation Rules, rule 8.7(a)				
• any material changes to relevant information about the practice including changes to key personnel, such as a manager, COLP or COFA, joining or leaving the practice or a merger with, or an acquisition by or of, another firm	SRA Authorisation Rules, rule 8.7(c) 2011 Code, O(10.3), IB(10.8)				
• any awareness or knowledge of information that reasonably suggests that the practice has or may have provided the SRA with information which was or may have been false, misleading, incomplete or inaccurate, or has or may have changed in a materially significant way	SRA Authorisation Rules, rule 8.7(d)				
• action taken against the practice by another regulator	2011 Code, O(10.3), IB(10.7)				

• serious misconduct by any person or firm authorised by the SRA, or any employee, manager or owner of any such firm (taking into account, where necessary, duty of confidentiality)	2011 Code, O(10.4)		
• In the event that the practice ceases to have a compliance officer, immediately and in any event within 7 days: – notify the SRA – designate another manager or employee to replace its previous compliance officer – make an application to the SRA for temporary approval of the new COFA	SRA Authorisation Rules, rule 18.1 Appendix C – Notification and temporary emergency approval application letter to the SRA		
• Where the compliance officer is likely to be absent for a significant length of time they may need to be replaced. The practice should discuss whether replacement is appropriate with their supervisory team at the SRA	Law Society practice note: Compliance officers, section 7		
5.2 Copies of all the information provided to SRA about the practice are kept in a central location and reviewed periodically so as to be able to consider whether there are any material changes that need to be communicated promptly to the SRA	2011 Code, O(10.3)		

Requirement	Source	Templates available in the toolkit	Procedure in place	Work performed to ensure procedure is operating effectively	Satisfactory/ Improvement required/No evidence
5.3 Contingency plans are in place for when nominated individuals are absent	Based on 2011 Code, IB(7.4) and SRA Authorisation Rules, rule 18				
6 Other requirements					
6.1 Consider whether individuals working in the administration and finance department have the level of competence appropriate to their work and level of responsibility and provide training as necessary	2011 Code, O(7.6)				
6.2 There is a whistle-blowing policy and all the employees, managers and principals of the firm are aware of the policy	2011 Code, IB(10.10)				
6.3 Arrangements are in place for the continuation of the business in the event of absences and emergencies, for example holiday or sick leave, with the minimum interruption to clients' business	2011 Code, IB(7.4)				

APPENDIX B

Terms of appointment to role of COFA

> **Note:** Illustrative wording to assist practices drafting terms of appointment to the role of COFA is provided below. Additional considerations may be necessary depending on the type of organisation. For example, practices with an overseas office will need to consider how the COFA will gain access to information kept overseas.

TERMS OF APPOINTMENT TO THE POSITION OF COMPLIANCE OFFICER FOR FINANCE AND ADMINISTRATION (COFA) OF [*NAME OF FIRM*] (THE FIRM) AND RECORD OF THE APPOINTED INDIVIDUAL'S ACCEPTANCE

On behalf of the Firm we hereby confirm that we will ensure that you will have access to the necessary information and that you will be granted the necessary authority to allow you to exercise effectively your responsibilities as COFA [*Consider access to any information held by overseas practice*]. This will include, but is not limited to, ensuring that you will be in a position to:

- have access to all accounting records and business information;
- carry out regular checks on the accounting systems;
- have access to all client files to be able to carry out file and ledger reviews;
- ensure that the reporting accountant has access to all the information needed to complete the accountant's report;
- take steps to ensure that breaches of the SRA Accounts Rules are remedied promptly;
- monitor, review and manage risks to compliance with the SRA Accounts Rules;
- report to the SRA any breach of the SRA Accounts Rules which is material either on its own or as part of a pattern;
- report, where appropriate, when the practice is in serious financial difficulties.

> **Note:** As the SRA's quick guide, 'Outcomes-focused regulation at a glance' implies that there is a role for the COFA in reporting when the practice is in serious financial difficulties, COFAs may therefore also need to consider whether they are able to access information on the practice's overall financial status and be in a position to make an assessment of that status.

We confirm that we will ensure that no manager or employee of the Firm obstructs you in your role as COFA and that you will have direct access to the Firm's [management committee/senior partner].

We hereby authorise you to report to the SRA any material breach of the SRA Accounts Rules or other matter which the SRA Authorisation Rules require should be reported by a COFA to the SRA and waive any right of action against you for damages or loss resulting from any such reports which are made in good faith even though it may subsequently transpire that you were mistaken in the belief that there was cause for concern.

We agree to provide you with an indemnity for any financial sanction and/or defence costs and/or disbursements arising from any investigation, inquiry and/or proceedings brought by the SRA against you personally arising from exercising the role of COFA provided that you have acted in good faith and with reasonable due care and attention.

Signed on behalf of the Firm

_____
Signature

_____
Name and position, printed

_____
Date

COFA's consent

I hereby accept appointment as the COFA of the Firm on the terms set out above and confirm that I have the necessary skills and experience to take on this role.

_____
Signature

_____
Name, printed

_____
Date

APPENDIX C

Notification and temporary emergency approval application letter to the SRA

[Firm's contact details]

Solicitors Regulation Authority
Ipsley Court
Berrington Close
Redditch
Worcestershire
B98 0TD

[Date]

Your ref: *[SRA ref]*

Our ref: *[internal ref]*

Dear Sirs,

We write to advise you that our existing COFA, *[name]*, is currently unable to fulfil [his/her] role due to *[set out circumstances]*. Therefore, in accordance with rule 18 of the SRA Authorisation Rules we are writing to notify you of our designation of *[name of temporary replacement]* as the COFA and hereby apply for temporary emergency approval of *[name of new COFA]*.

Please acknowledge receipt of this notification with confirmation that temporary approval has been granted.

We look forward to hearing from you.

Yours faithfully

APPENDIX D

SRA guidelines – accounting procedures and systems checklist

> **Notes:** The following checklist based on Appendix 3 to the SRA Accounts Rules should assist the COFA when monitoring compliance with the SRA's guidelines on dealings with client money and the SRA Accounts Rules. Adherence to these guidelines, however, does not obviate the need to comply fully with the SRA Accounts Rules. It is therefore recommended that as well as completing and reviewing this checklist on a regular basis, practices also consider maintaining a full list of the SRA Accounts Rules, showing how each individual requirement has been addressed.

Guideline	Procedure/ policy in place	Work performed to ensure procedure is operating effectively	Document reference	Satisfactory/ Improvement required/No evidence
A General				
A1. The practice should hold a copy of the current version of the SRA Accounts Rules and/or have ready access to the current online version				
A2. The person who maintains the books of account must have a full knowledge of the requirements of the rules and the accounting requirements of the practice				
A3. Proper books of account should be maintained on the double-entry principle. They should be legible, up to date and contain narratives with the entries which identify and/or provide adequate information about the transaction				
A4. Entries to the books of account should be made in chronological order and the current balance should be shown on the client ledger accounts or be readily ascertainable in accordance with rule 29.9				

Guideline	Procedure/ policy in place	Work performed to ensure procedure is operating effectively	Document reference	Satisfactory/ Improvement required/No evidence
A5. Ledger accounts for clients, other persons or trusts should include the name of the client or other person or trust and contain a heading which provides a description of the matter or transaction				
A6. When introducing new systems, care must be taken to ensure: 1. that balances transferred from the old to the new system are reconciled before day-to-day operation commences 2. that the new system operates correctly before the old system is abandoned (this may require parallel running of both systems until the reconciliation is completed)				
A7. Office account entries are maintained up to date in relation to each client or trust matter				
A8. Credit balances on office account are fully investigated				
A9. There are policies and systems in operation to ensure the payment of fair and reasonable interest to clients in accordance with rules 22 and 23				
A10. The terms of the policy must be drawn to the attention of the client at the outset of a retainer, unless it is inappropriate to do so in the circumstances				
B Receipt of client money				
B1. There are procedures for identifying client money whether received through post, electronically or direct by personnel and for promptly recording the receipt of the money either in the books of account or in a register for later posting to the client cash book and ledger accounts				
B2. Client money is kept safely prior to banking				

Guideline	Procedure/ policy in place	Work performed to ensure procedure is operating effectively	Document reference	Satisfactory/ Improvement required/No evidence
B3. There are procedures to ensure that client money is paid promptly into a client account				
B4. There is a system for identifying money which should not be in a client account and transferring it without delay				
B5. There is a policy and a system in place for dealing with mixed monies in compliance with rules 17–19	An example of a policy dealing with mixed monies is provided in **Appendix J**			
B6. There are procedures for ensuring that client money in a currency other than sterling is held in a separate account for the appropriate currency, and that separate books of account for that currency are kept				
C Payments from client account				
C1. There are clear procedures for ensuring that all withdrawals from client accounts are properly authorised				
C2. Suitable persons should be named for authorisation of the following: 1. Authorisation of internal payment vouchers 2. Signing client account cheques 3. Authorising telegraphic or electronic transfers No other personnel should be allowed to authorise or sign the documents				
C3. There are procedures and systems to ensure that those persons permitted to authorise the withdrawal of client money from a client account have an appropriate understanding of the requirements of the rules, including rules 20 and 21, which set out when and how a withdrawal from a client account may be properly made				

Guideline	Procedure/ policy in place	Work performed to ensure procedure is operating effectively	Document reference	Satisfactory/ Improvement required/No evidence
C4. Persons nominated for the purpose of authorising internal payment vouchers should, for each payment, ensure that there is supporting evidence showing clearly the reason for the payment, and the date of it				
C5. Persons signing cheques and authorising transfers should ensure that there is a suitable voucher or other supporting evidence to support the payment				
C6. There are systems and procedures for authorising electronic withdrawals from client accounts with appropriate safeguards and controls to ensure that all such withdrawals are properly authorised				
C7. There are systems and procedures in place for ensuring that debit balances do not arise on client ledgers				
C8. Where payments are to be made other than out of cleared funds, clear policies and procedures are in place to ensure that adequate risk assessment is applied				
C9. A system is in place for the transfer of costs from client account to office account in accordance with rule 17.2 and 17.3				
C10. Policies and systems are in place to control and record accurately any transfers between clients of the firm. Where these arise as a result of loans between clients, the written authority of both the lender and borrower must be obtained in accordance with rule 27.2				
C11. There are policies and procedures to ensure the timely closure of files				
C12. There are policies and a system in place for the prompt accounting for surplus balances in accordance with rule 14.3				

Guideline	Procedure/ policy in place	Work performed to ensure procedure is operating effectively	Document reference	Satisfactory/ Improvement required/No evidence
C13. There are systems in accordance with rule 14.4 to keep clients regularly informed when funds are retained for a specified reason at the end of a matter or the substantial conclusion of a matter				
D Overall control of client accounts				
D1. The firm maintains control of all its bank and building society accounts opened for the purpose of holding client money. In the case of a joint account, a suitable degree of control should be exercised				
D2. Central records or central registers are kept in respect of: 1. Accounts held for client money, which are not client accounts (rules 15.1(a), 16.1(d) and 29.19) 2. Practice as a liquidator, trustee in bankruptcy, Court of Protection deputy, or trustee of an occupational scheme (rules 8 and 29.20) 3. Joint accounts (rules 9 and 29.21) 4. Dividend payments received by an executor, trustee or nominee company as nominee (rules 28.2 and 29.23) 5. Clients' own accounts (rules 10, 15.1(b) and 30.3)				
D3. There is a master list of all: • General client accounts • Separate designated client accounts • Accounts held in respect of D2 above • Office accounts The master list shows the current status of each account, e.g. currently in operation or closed with date of closure				

Guideline	Procedure/ policy in place	Work performed to ensure procedure is operating effectively	Document reference	Satisfactory/ Improvement required/No evidence
D4. The firm operates a system to ensure that accurate reconciliations of client accounts are carried out at least every five weeks. In particular it ensures that: 1. A full list of client ledger balances is produced. Any debit balances are listed, fully investigated and rectified immediately. The total of any debit balances cannot be 'netted off' against the total of credit balances 2. A full list of unpresented cheques is produced 3. A list of outstanding lodgements is produced 4. Formal statements are produced, reconciling the client cash book balances, aggregate client ledger balances and the client bank accounts. All unresolved differences are investigated and, where appropriate, corrective action taken 5. A manager or the COFA checks the reconciliation statement and any corrective action, and ensures that enquiries are made into any unusual or apparently unsatisfactory items or still unresolved matters				
D5. There are clear policies, systems and procedures to control access to computerised client accounts that determine the personnel who should have 'write to' and 'read only' access				
D6. Passwords are held confidentially by designated personnel and changed regularly to maintain security				

Guideline	Procedure/ policy in place	Work performed to ensure procedure is operating effectively	Document reference	Satisfactory/ Improvement required/No evidence
D7. Policies and systems for the retention of the accounting records ensure that: • Books of account, reconciliations, bills, bank statements and passbooks are kept for at least six years • Paid cheques, digital images of paid cheques and other authorities for the withdrawal of money from a client account are kept for at least two years • Other vouchers and internal expenditure authorisation documents relating directly to entries in the client account books are kept for at least two years				
D8. Unused client account cheques are stored securely to prevent unauthorised access. Blank cheques are not pre-signed and any cancelled cheques are retained				

APPENDIX E

Guidance on matter file reviews

The guidance in this appendix is divided into three sections:

- Guidance on matter file documentation
- Matter file selection
- Matter file review process

The first section can be used by the COFA to benchmark the practice's current documentation policies and guidance and consider whether recommendations for improvement can be made.

1 Guidance on matter file documentation

The effect of the SRA Accounts Rules is to require documentation to be kept justifying all client money transactions. The SRA Accounts Rules do not however specify where this information needs to be maintained and so it is not a breach if some or all of the documentation is maintained outside the matter files, for example in the finance department. Best practice is to maintain at least the following types of documents on matter files (either manually or in electronic format). Where an authorised body departs from what is suggested in this document, the COFA should consider whether recommendations for improvement should be made to the fee earners. The list below should therefore only be used as the basis for any recommendations for improvement and not as authoritative guidance on what the SRA considers should go on matter files.

1.1 Transactions involving client monies

Best practice would require appropriate evidence for any transaction involving client monies.

1.2 Internal advice notes

Internal advice notes for receipts, payments and transfers should indicate the following:

- Date of transaction
- Client matter numbers involved in the transaction

- Name of the qualified solicitor responsible for the transaction (in the form of signature or initials)
- Explanation of the transaction either shown on the internal advice note or attached to it

Detailed documentation to be held on the matter file by transaction type.

1.3 Client to office transfers

Payment against a bill

- Copy of the bill as issued
- Copy of the written documentation stating intention that client monies are to be used against the bill sent to the client. (This may be shown on the bill or in a separate document.)
- Written documentation from the client informing the solicitor that funds may be used against costs
- Internal transfer advice, as above

Other

- Written authorisation from the client or copy of written communication from the solicitor to the client acknowledging that authorisation was received in another form
- Written notification from the solicitor indicating the proposed use of the funds
- Internal transfer advice, as above
- Relevant third party information

1.4 Office to client transfers

Interest payments

- Evidence that the firm's interest policy has been communicated to the client
- Copy of bank's/internal calculation of interest to be credited
- Written notification to client of amounts credited

Other

- Internal transfer advice, as above

1.5 Client to client transfers

To an unrelated matter

- Written notification from both clients authorising the transfer
- Written documentation giving reason for the transfer

- Third party evidence supporting reason for transfer
- Internal transfer advice, as above

To a related matter

- Written documentation giving reason for the transfer
- Third party evidence supporting reason for the transfer
- Internal transfer advice, as above
- Where the solicitor holds authority to transfer funds around related matters for a client, this authority must be held on file

1.6 Receipts into client account

- Written notification from client stating what the money is for
- Written notification from the third party describing the nature and amount of receipt
- Internal receipt advice, as above

1.7 Payments from client account

- Written notification from the solicitors to the client detailing the nature of the payment
- Relevant third party correspondence detailing the nature of the transaction and due dates of payment if relevant
- Written third party acknowledgement of receipt
- Internal payment advice, as above

2 Matter file selection

The COFA should consider skewing the selection of matter files towards the following:

- Matter files belonging to managers that have left during the period under review
- Matter files belonging to newly promoted managers in their second year (on the principle that they will not hold substantial client money in their first year)
- Matter files belonging to all laterally hired managers in their first year
- Matter files relating to any new areas of the business
- Matter files belonging to managers who hold the majority of client money on a rotational basis (every three years recommended)
- Matter files where the COFA has become aware of potential breaches of the SRA Accounts Rules by indirect means
- Matter files belonging to other managers on a rotational basis

The final selection should be a balanced reflection of the firm's practices for the period under review.

3   Matter file review process

Once the file selection process is complete, the COFA should oversee a review of all system transactions processed through the client and office accounts for each matter in the period under review. Comparison should be made to ensure that the transactions recorded on each ledger are adequately supported by documentation on the matter file. Any breaches of the SRA Accounts Rules noted as a result of this review should be documented and held on record in compliance with the SRA Authorisation Rules.

The matter file review template provided in **Appendix F** can be used to document matter file reviews and resulting conclusions. It is suggested that each transaction of both client and office ledger within the review period is noted chronologically within the review form so as to ensure completeness. Key pointers in the review process are as follows:

- Document the reason/purpose for the matter file, including the names and addresses of the main parties involved.
- Check the cast of each client ledger account.
- Verify that no payments have been made from client account in excess of the monies held on that account (i.e. that the client account was not overdrawn at any time).
- From inspection of correspondence and other documents in the client file, document the reason for each transaction and ascertain whether the entries in the client ledger accounts correctly reflect the transactions in a manner complying with the SRA Accounts Rules, distinguishing between client and office money:

  - Verify that all client monies invested other than in a normal client account have been authorised by the client in writing.
  - Trace to the accounting records any amounts which, according to documentation on the client file, have been paid to or by the solicitor (on behalf of the client) and ascertain whether the transactions have been made in compliance with the SRA Accounts Rules.
  - Confirm that dates correspond with cash diaries.
  - Confirm that receipts have been paid into client account without delay.
  - Where clients' money has been deposited in a separate designated account confirm that the item appears in the ledger in a separate designated deposit account.
  - Check that all transfers from client to office accounts comply with the SRA Accounts Rules, rule 17.

- Review the client ledger and check that every transaction has been agreed to the client file, preferably to third party correspondence. Investigate the reason for all transactions not referred to in the client file.
- Obtain explanations of entries in the ledger accounts which are not referred to in the client file.

- Where the matter relates to a conveyancing transaction and the solicitor is acting for both borrower and lender, and maintaining only one ledger account as permitted by the SRA Accounts Rules, rule 29.10, confirm that the funds belonging to each party are clearly identifiable and that the lender is an institutional lender which provides mortgages on standard terms in the normal course of its activities.
- Where a matter is complete, confirm that any residual balance has been returned to the client promptly and where such attempts have failed, that the client has been re-informed of the balance at least annually in compliance with the SRA Accounts Rules, rule 14.4.

APPENDIX F

Matter file review template

Individual responsible for the matter file:	
Client name:	
Matter number:	
Reason for matter file:	*[fully understand and document terms of engagement, status of matter file and any known disputes between the firm and the client through delivery of the engagement]*
Engagement letter on file?	Yes/No

Reference to ledger*	Date	Reason for transactions	Evidence on file supporting transaction
A			
B			
C			
D			
E			
F			
G [etc.]			

* It is recommended that a copy of the matter ledger is put on file alongside the completed review template and cross-references made to the transactions discussed, either through use of alphabetical references or otherwise.

Client monies remaining on client account:

[SRA Accounts Rules, rule 14 – where client monies remain on client account and the matter is not ongoing/there have been no movements on client account for over 12 months, address the considerations of rule 14 as to whether:
- *prompt attempts to return client monies have been made; and*
- *the client has been informed at least annually of any residual balance on a completed matter.]*

Summary of breaches noted:

[*Summarise any breaches noted*]

Steps taken to remedy any such breaches:

[*Summarise steps taken where applicable*]

Remedial actions to reduce the risk of such breaches reoccurring in the future:

[*e.g. modification of systems and procedures or additional staff training*]

Conclusion:

[*Conclude on status of any breaches noted – material/non-material and note date of reporting to SRA where applicable*]

Proforma templates for the recording of breaches internally

> Note: The following two tables are proforma templates to record any breaches noted.

Recording of material breaches

Material breaches reported to the SRA under SRA Authorisation Rules, rule 8.5(e) occurring within the period from [XX] to [XX]

Date breach noted	Date breach corrected (if applicable)	Rule(s) breached?	Number of instances of breach noted?	Monetary amounts involved (currency)	Description of breach	Steps taken to rectify error or control deficiency leading to breach	Details of any disciplinary action taken as a result of discovery of breach	Basis for reporting to SRA*	Date of letter to SRA reporting breach
Example: Breaches of the SRA Accounts Rules									
12/4/12	14/4/12	SRA Accounts Rules, rule 14.4	25	Total value of £24,500	Following COFA review of a sample of matters where balances on client account had not moved in over 12 months, 25 instances were noted in respect of completed matters where the fee earners had not informed the respective clients at least annually of the residual balances on account.	Fee earners now receive monthly prompts by e-mail to alert them to their client account balances on closed matters. These reports are monitored and chasers sent.	None as formal procedures were not in place at the time of the breach.	Volume of instances	14/4/12
Breaches of other SRA regulatory requirements									

* This should be consistent with the information reported to the SRA.

Recording of 'non-material' breaches

Non-material breaches noted by the COFA and recorded internally for reporting under the SRA authorisation process occurring within the period from [XX] to [XX]

Date breach noted	Date breach corrected (if applicable)	Rule(s) breached?	Monetary amounts involved (currency)	Description of breach	Steps taken to rectify error or control deficiency leading to breach	Rationale behind classification as 'non-material'	Confirm with reference to previously noted breaches on this form that there is no evidence of a developing pattern that would indicate elevation to a 'material' breach
Example: Breaches of the SRA Accounts Rules							
8/4/12	8/4/12	14.1	£1,500	A cheque representing client money was received on 3/4/12 but not banked until 8/4/12. This delay breaches the 'without delay' guideline within the rule. The breach arose because the cheque remained on the fee earner's desk for a couple of days before being passed to the accounts department.	Systems are already in place to ensure that cheques received by post are ordinarily passed to the accounts department.	This cheque was a one-off and was received by hand. Ordinarily a partner would immediately pass this to a secretary to deliver to accounts; however the concerned partner's secretary was on holiday on this specific day. Breach therefore as a result of a one-off, human error and no pervasive risk is noted.	Confirmed
Breaches of other SRA regulatory requirements							

APPENDIX H

Template letter for reporting material breaches to the SRA

> **Note:** This template letter for reporting material breaches to the SRA is provided by way of example only to provide guidance as to the key components to appear in the body of the text. The example relates to breach(es) of the SRA Accounts Rules, but can be tailored to address different types of non-compliance. Practices should ensure that they comply fully with the SRA Handbook in disclosing all relevant details.

[Firm's contact details]

Solicitors Regulation Authority
Ipsley Court
Berrington Close
Redditch
Worcestershire
B98 0TD

[Date]

Your ref: *[SRA ref]*

Our ref: *[internal ref]*

Dear Sirs,

As required under rule 8.5(e) of the SRA Authorisation Rules, and in my role as COFA for *[name of firm]* I am writing to inform you of the following material failure to comply with the SRA Accounts Rules, rule *[xx]* that has come to my attention within our practice.

The failure has been deemed material on account of [the volume of instances of non-compliance with rule *[xx]* noted]/[the resulting detriment or risk of detriment to a client]/[the scale of the issue]/[the overall impact on the practice, its clients and third parties that it has had].

The history of the breach[es] giving rise to this failure is set out below:

[Provide succinct history covering:

- *Timing of breach(es) and discovery*
- *Nature of breach(es); quoting number of rule breached and any quantifiable amounts*
- *Whether breach(es) resulted in any loss to a client*
- *Cause of breach(es)*
- *Status of rectification of error/deficiency in control giving rise to breach(es) (if applicable)*
- *Any recompense given to clients*
- *Any disciplinary action taken as a result of breach(es) or remedial action(s) to reduce the risk of reoccurrence in the future*]

Should you require any further information in respect of the above matter please do not hesitate to contact me.

Yours sincerely,

[Signature of COFA]

[Printed name and position of COFA]

APPENDIX I

Common areas of breaches of the SRA Accounts Rules

General

Rule 12.8 (extract): Matters in the sole name of partner (or firm where the firm is an LLP)

> If a firm conducts a personal or office transaction – for instance, conveyancing – for a principal (or for a number of principals), money held or received on behalf of the principal(s) is office money ...

(i.e. all dealings with this money should be recorded through the office ledger.)

Client money and operation of a client account

Rule 13.3 (extract): Client bank accounts naming convention

> ... the name of the [client] account must also include the word 'client' in full (an abbreviation is not acceptable).

Rule 14.1: Depositing of client money 'without delay'

> Client money must without delay be paid into a client account, and must be held in a client account, except when the rules provide to the contrary (see rules, 8, 9, 15, 16, 17 and 19).

(N.B. 'Without delay' is defined in the SRA Handbook Glossary as meaning 'in normal circumstances, either on the day of receipt or on the next working day'.)

Rule 14.3: Prompt return of residual balances

> Client money must be returned to the client (or other person on whose behalf the money is held) promptly, as soon as there is no longer any proper reason to retain those funds. Payments received after you have already accounted to the client, for example by way of a refund, must be paid to the client promptly.

(N.B. 'Promptly' is not officially defined but on review of a file, challenges should be raised by the COFA where the delay exceeds one calendar month from the date of completion of the matter.)

Rule 14.4: Re-informing clients of residual balances

> You must promptly inform a client (or other person on whose behalf the money is held) in writing of the amount of any client money retained at the end of a matter (or the substantial conclusion of a matter), and the reason for that retention. You must inform the client (or other person) in writing at least once every twelve months thereafter of the amount of client money still held and the reason for the retention, for as long as you continue to hold that money.

(N.B. See above for consideration of 'promptly'.)

Rule 17.1(b)(ii): Treatment of receipts which include monies relating to unpaid professional disbursements

Where such mixed monies receipts are paid initially into office account under rule 17.1(b)(i):

> by the end of the second working day following receipt, either pay any unpaid professional disbursement, or transfer a sum for its settlement to a client account ...

Rule 17.2 and 17.3: Receipt of monies in settlement of your costs

These rules have been grouped together because within the new SRA Accounts Rules, they are now interlinked for clarity (refer to guidance note (viii) to rule 17).

> 17.2 If you properly require payment of your fees from money held for a client or trust in a client account, you must first give or send a bill of costs, or other written notification of the costs incurred, to the client or the paying party.
>
> 17.3 Once you have complied with rule 17.2 above, the money earmarked for costs becomes office money and must be transferred out of the client account within 14 days.

Rule 20.1 (extracts): Withdrawals from a client account where there is no 'proper requirement' or 'written confirmation'

> Client money may only be withdrawn from a client account when it is:
>
> (a)   properly required for a payment to or on behalf of the client (or other person on whose behalf the money is being held) ...
>
> (f)   withdrawn on the client's instructions, provided the instructions are for the client's convenience and are given in writing, or are given by other means and confirmed by you to the client in writing;

(N.B. There are other elements to this rule but these are the most common areas of non-compliance.)

Rule 21.1: Specific authority for withdrawal from client account

A withdrawal from a client account may be made only after a specific authority in respect of that withdrawal has been signed by an appropriate person or persons in accordance with the firm's procedures for signing on client account. An authority for withdrawals from client account may be signed electronically, subject to appropriate safeguards and controls.

(N.B. This rule is new within the SRA Accounts Rules and should be attended to.)

Interest

Due consideration should be given to the changes to the rules governing the application of interest to client balances retained by the authorised body. Non-familiarity with these changes could result in a reportable breach.

Rule 22.1 (extract): Accounting for interest on client balances

When you hold money in a client account for a client, or for a person funding all or part of your fees, or for a trust, you must account to the client or that person or trust for interest when it is fair and reasonable to do so in all the circumstances. ...

(N.B. There is no formal definition given to 'fair and reasonable' within the rules but it is expected that this should draw on the actual rates of interest being earned on the client accounts. For the avoidance of doubt, a de minimis of £20 for the accrual of interest would generally continue to be acceptable in the absence of any unusual circumstances.)

Rule 22.3: A written policy on the payment of interest

You must have a written policy on the payment of interest, which seeks to provide a fair outcome. The terms of the policy must be drawn to the attention of the client at the outset of a retainer, unless it is inappropriate to do so in the circumstances.

(N.B. It is recommended that this policy be built into the communication of the terms of engagement given at the outset of every new client matter.)

Accounting systems and records

Rule 29.1 and 29.2: Up-to-date and appropriate accounting records

29.1 You must at all times keep accounting records properly written up to show your dealings with:

   (a) client money received, held or paid by you; including client money held outside a client account under rule 15.1(a) or rule 16.1(d); and
   (b) any office money relating to any client or trust matter.

29.2 All dealings with client money must be appropriately recorded:

(a) in a client cash account or in a record of sums transferred from one client ledger account to another; and

(b) on the client side of a separate client ledger account for each client (or other person, or trust).

Rule 29.12: Frequency and completeness of reconciliations

You must, at least once every five weeks:

(a) compare the balance on the client cash account(s) with the balances shown on the statements and passbooks (after allowing for all unpresented items) of all general client accounts and separate designated client accounts, and of any account which is not a client account but in which you hold client money under rule 15.1(a) or rule 16.1(d), and any client money held by you in cash; and

(b) as at the same date prepare a listing of all the balances shown by the client ledger accounts of the liabilities to clients (and other persons, and trusts) and compare the total of those balances with the balance on the client cash account; and also

(c) prepare a reconciliation statement; this statement must show the cause of the difference, if any, shown by each of the above comparisons.

(N.B. There should be evidence of review of the client account reconciliations by someone with overall authority, if not by the COFA themselves.)

Rule 29.25: Suspense ledger accounts

Suspense client ledger accounts may be used only when you can justify their use; for instance, for temporary use on receipt of an unidentified payment, if time is needed to establish the nature of the payment or the identity of the client.

(N.B. 'Temporary use' is not officially defined but in general a breach would be noted where a balance remains in suspense in excess of one calendar month.)

Guidance note (vii) to rule 29

Solicitors or recognised bodies are permitted to:

... include on a bill of costs any disbursements which have been properly incurred but not paid before delivery of the bill, subject to those disbursements being described on the bill as unpaid.

APPENDIX J

Example of internal policy for dealing with mixed payments

Rules 17–19 of the SRA Accounts Rules require certain behaviours in respect of receipt and dealings with mixed payments. The policy below is designed to act as a guide to practices when drafting their own internal policies so as to ensure compliance with the rules. It should be adapted where necessary to complement any bespoke systems that the practice has in place.

Receipt and transfer of costs

When [*name of firm*] receives money paid in full or part settlement of our bill(s) (or other notification(s) of cost) we deal with the payment as follows.

On the same working day as the day of receipt, we determine the composition of the payment and:

(i)   if the sum comprises office money and/or out-of-scope money, as defined by the SRA Accounts Rules, we place it direct into an office account;
(ii) if the sum comprises only client money, as defined by the SRA Accounts Rules, we place the entire sum into a client account (we note that it is not acceptable to place payments comprising only client money into an office account, regardless of whether this money is then transferred out on the same working day); and
(iii) if the sum includes both office money and client money, or client money and out-of-scope money, or all three, we deal with it as 'a mixed payment' and follow the procedures detailed below.

Receipt of mixed payments

Where the mixed payment contains client money other than that relating to unpaid professional disbursements we place the entire sum into a client account on the date of receipt, or on the next working day and transfer any office money and/or out-of-scope money out of the client account within 14 days of receipt.

Where the mixed payment comprises office money and/or out-of-scope money *and* client money in the form of professional disbursements incurred but not yet paid, we:

[*Option 1:*

(i)   place the entire sum into an English or Welsh based office account and by the end of the second working day following receipt, either:

(a) pay any unpaid professional disbursement; or
(b) transfer a sum for its settlement to a client account.]

[*Option 2:*

(i)   place the entire sum into a client account on the date of receipt, or on the next working day and transfer any office money and/or out-of-scope money out of the client account within 14 days of receipt; or
(ii) in the event that monies comprise receipt of non-regular costs from the Legal Services Commission, place these receipts into office account and by the end of the second working day following receipt, either:

(a) pay any unpaid professional disbursement; or
(b) transfer a sum for its settlement to a client account.

(N.B. Where we receive regular payments from the Legal Services Commission, we pay these direct into office account).]

In the event that monies comprise a cheque in respect of damages and costs, made payable to the client, we bank this into client account under the Society's Conditional Fee Agreement and transfer any office money and/or out-of-scope money out of the client account within 14 days of receipt.

This policy will be reviewed annually on [*date*] by [*name of relevant member in senior management team*] as part of the ongoing review of compliance with the SRA Accounts Rules required by the SRA Handbook.

APPENDIX K

Framework for monitoring, reviewing and managing risks of non-compliance

The 2011 Code requires practices to have effective systems and controls to enable them to meet the requirements of the Code.

As part of the management of the business, risks of non-compliance with regulatory requirements and other risks need to be identified and their significance to the practice assessed. This is usually done by considering the probability of the risk occurring and its impact on the practice. The higher the probability of the risk occurring and the higher its impact, the more significant the risk is.

The risks to be considered by practices will vary depending on their size and nature and the type of work undertaken, but would generally cover financial, operational and business continuity matters. Risks likely to be relevant to most practices include:

- Risks of non-compliance with the requirements of the SRA Handbook
- Risks to the financial stability of the practice, credit risks and exposure
- Risks to money and assets entrusted by clients and others
- Complaints and claims under legislation relating to matters such as data protection, IT failures and abuses, and damage to offices
- Risks from operating overseas (where applicable)

The systems in place to identify and assess risks will vary depending on the size and complexity of the practice and may range from simple brainstorming sessions to more systematic approaches. Once the risks have been identified and assessed, the practice needs to consider whether there are adequate systems and controls in place to mitigate the risks and check at regular intervals that they are operating effectively.

Note: The table below provides an example of a framework to assist practices in monitoring, reviewing and managing risks as part of their consideration of the effectiveness of their compliance arrangements.

Risk management framework

Risk description	Potential impact of the risk on the practice [low, medium, high]	Probability of the risk [low, medium, high]	Overall risk [low, medium, high]	Controls/ systems to mitigate the risk	Individual responsible for mitigation of the risk [name, position, qualification]	Monitoring the effectiveness of the controls/ systems to mitigate the risk

The graphic below provides an example of a visual representation of a risk map.

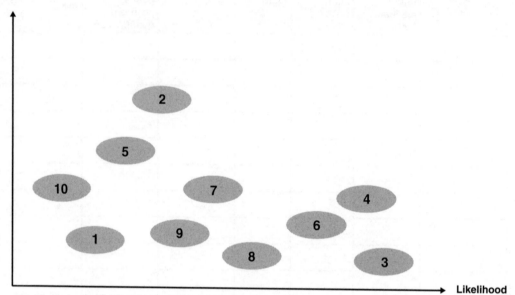

1. [*Label risk*]
2. [*Label risk*]
3. [*Label risk*]
4. [*Label risk*]
5. [*Label risk*]
6. [*Label risk*]
7. [*Label risk*]
8. [*Label risk*]
9. [*Label risk*]
10. [*Label risk*]

APPENDIX L

Examples of key general controls expected to be in place in law firms

The table below provides a template to document key controls, what the controls have been designed to achieve, how they have been implemented and to test the operating effectiveness of these controls. The table includes examples of some of the key general controls that would be expected to be found within a law firm. It is not a complete list of all the key controls that would be expected to be in place and it should be tailored to the particular circumstances of the firm, adding additional controls if necessary.

Ref	Key control activity	Control type (automatic/ manual/ policy)	Control in place (yes/ no/N/A)	Control frequency	Sample size	Is the control appropriately designed to mitigate the risk and has it been implemented as designed?	Testing – has the control operated effectively during the period?	Satisfactory/ Unsatisfactory?	Comments/ recommend-ations for improvement
1 Governance assessment									
1.1 Governance mechanisms									
1.1.1	Staff have access to the firm's policies and procedure manuals.								
1.1.2	There is a division of responsibilities and segregation of duties that is appropriate for the size and nature of the business.								

Ref	Key control activity	Control type (automatic/ manual/ policy)	Control in place (yes/ no/N/A)	Control frequency	Sample size	Is the control appropriately designed to mitigate the risk and has it been implemented as designed?	Testing – has the control operated effectively during the period?	Satisfactory/ Unsatisfactory?	Comments/ recommend- ations for improvement
1.1.3	Delegated authority limits are documented and have been approved by the appropriate authority and local financial mandates comply with firm-approved limits. Sample signatures of all authorising individuals are held on file.								
1.1.4	Formal processes exist which set out authority limits and documentation requirements over the following areas: capital expenditure, staff appointments and the issue of company cars.								
1.1.5	Budgets and forecasts are produced on at least an annual basis and reviewed by management against actuals on a regular basis. Amendments to these forecasts are then made in line with actual trends.								

1.1.6	Formal processes exist to ensure compliance with the terms of any financial or informational bank covenants.				
1.2 Compliance					
1.2.1	Local senior management are aware of the requirements of the SRA Accounts Rules and staff are placed on training programmes to keep them updated on the requirements regarding client money.				
2 Expenditure					
2.1 Masterfile data					
2.1.1	All amendments to supplier masterfile have been authorised by the appropriate level of management and a monthly report of all changes has been produced, independently checked, authorised and retained.				

Ref	Key control activity	Control type (automatic/manual/policy)	Control in place (yes/no/N/A)	Control frequency	Sample size	Is the control appropriately designed to mitigate the risk and has it been implemented as designed?	Testing – has the control operated effectively during the period?	Satisfactory/ Unsatisfactory?	Comments/ recommend-ations for improvement
2.2 Order authorisation									
2.2.1	Purchase orders are sequentially numbered and placed only with appropriate level of authorisation (according to a formalised authority schedule).								
2.2.2	All invoices for non-purchase order goods/services (i.e. those not pre-authorised) are authorised prior to payment according to a formalised authority schedule.								
2.3 Accounts payable									
2.3.1	Management review expenditure made on a regular basis through comparison with budget. Variances are highlighted and explanations sought.								

Ref	Control					
2.3.2	An aged creditors listing is maintained and reviewed by management on a timely basis.					
3 Sales and receivables						
3.1 Customer acceptance						
3.1.1	Before client engagements are accepted, conflict checks, money laundering checks and other risk assessments are completed.					
3.1.2	An up-to-date engagement letter is in place which states clearly the parties to the engagement and the scope of the work completed.					
3.2 Billing						
3.2.1	Bills are raised based on benchmark rates or agreed fees clearly stated in the engagement letter. All discounts/write-offs on bills raised are authorised in accordance with a formalised authority schedule.					
3.2.2	Bill are approved and reviewed by partners before being sent out to clients and recorded.					

Ref	Key control activity	Control type (automatic/ manual/ policy)	Control in place (yes/ no/N/A)	Control frequency	Sample size	Is the control appropriately designed to mitigate the risk and has it been implemented as designed?	Testing – has the control operated effectively during the period?	Satisfactory/ Unsatisfactory?	Comments/ recommend-ations for improvement
3.3 Masterfile data									
3.3.1	Any changes in the client's details (i.e. billing address, client name) are authorised by a fee earner and have been agreed to appropriate backup.								
3.4 Accounts receivable									
3.4.1	Overdue receivable balances are reviewed on a regular basis and chasing actions recorded.								
3.4.2	An aged receivable listing is reviewed by management on a timely basis and longstanding receivable balances are reviewed and escalated.								
3.4.3	A review of the adequacy of any bad debt provision is performed on a timely basis by management and appropriate follow-up action taken.								

3.5 Credit notes							
3.5.1	All credit notes are approved by the partner and are raised for an appropriate and valid reason within firm-approved authorisation limits.						
3.5.2	A monthly report of credit notes raised is reviewed by management at month end.						
4 Treasury cash and banking							
4.1 Banking arrangements							
4.1.1	An up-to-date bank mandate is held for each bank account which requires instructions to be approved by two authorised signatures.						
4.1.2	Bank reconciliations are performed for each bank account on at least a monthly basis and are reviewed by management. Differences are investigated and actioned.						
4.1.3	All cash is deposited with firm-approved counterparties.						

Ref	Key control activity	Control type (automatic/ manual/ policy)	Control in place (yes/ no/N/A)	Control frequency	Sample size	Is the control appropriately designed to mitigate the risk and has it been implemented as designed?	Testing – has the control operated effectively during the period?	Satisfactory/ Unsatisfactory?	Comments/ recommend- ations for improvement
4.2 Payments									
4.2.1	All payment runs, including cheque payments and electronic funds transfers, are supported by appropriate banking documentation and authorised (per a formalised authority schedule) prior to release.								
4.3 Foreign exchange									
4.3.1	All trading and hedging transactions and balances are within limits authorised by an appropriate level of management.								
4.4 Petty cash balances and cheques									
4.4.1	Cash balances and cheques are held in a physically secure location.								
4.4.2	Cash balances are completely and accurately recorded and are reconciled every month.								

4.4.3	Petty cash payments to employees for small purchases are documented and authorised by a responsible official and cash amounts signed for by the employee.			
4.5 Client money				
4.5.1	Client money is separately distinguished from office money. Money is maintained within a separate client account. Reconciliations are performed at least every five weeks.			
4.5.2	Client account complies with the SRA Accounts Rules, an audit of which is completed on a yearly basis. If the report is qualified, qualifications are investigated and actions implemented to ensure no further qualifications.			

Ref	Key control activity	Control type (automatic/ manual/ policy)	Control in place (yes/ no/N/A)	Control frequency	Sample size	Is the control appropriately designed to mitigate the risk and has it been implemented as designed?	Testing – has the control operated effectively during the period?	Satisfactory/ Unsatisfactory?	Comments/ recommend- ations for improvement
5 Work in progress									
5.1 Timesheets									
5.1.1	All staff and partners complete timesheets on a regular basis. Timesheets are reviewed on a regular basis and alerts are sent to those not having fully completed their timesheet. This ensures that all time is captured on the system for the purposes of billing.								
5.2 WIP									
5.2.1	A monthly review of the WIP balances is completed on matters with each matter partner. As part of this review, the recoverability of the WIP balance is assessed and where applicable bills raised or WIP written off.								

6 Property, plant and equipment						
6.1 Fixed asset register						
6.1.1	Each asset has a unique reference number and a detailed and comprehensive asset register is maintained with a detailed description of each asset and details of cost, asset life and depreciation.					
6.2 Additions and disposals						
6.2.1	All fixed asset capital expenditure, including IT capital expenditure, is subject to assessment/appraisal and formalised authorisation procedures in accordance with the firm's policy.					
6.2.2	Disposals and write-offs are approved in accordance with the firm's procedures.					
6.3 Physical security and verification						
6.3.1	Formal processes are in place for asset verification, valuation and utilisation and fixed asset register is up to date to reflect these processes.					

Ref	Key control activity	Control type (automatic/ manual/ policy)	Control in place (yes/ no/N/A)	Control frequency	Sample size	Is the control appropriately designed to mitigate the risk and has it been implemented as designed?	Testing – has the control operated effectively during the period?	Satisfactory/ Unsatisfactory?	Comments/ recommend-ations for improvement
7 General accounting									
7.1 Month-end postings									
7.1.1	All manual journals are independently reviewed each month with evidence maintained of such review.								
7.2 Month-end close and submission									
7.2.1	The management accounts are derived from the trial balance. Any differences between the trial balance and the management accounts have been reviewed and reconciled with appropriate explanation provided for any reconciling items.								

7.2.2	For components of groups: The local management accounts reconcile to the position reported to group on a monthly basis. Any differences have been reviewed and appropriate explanation provided.		
7.2.3	Inter-company accounts are reconciled on a monthly basis. Disputed items have been recorded and resolved within a reasonable period.		
7.2.4	Month-end reconciliations are prepared for the below control accounts, with a documented review by management. Reconciliations to include but not be limited to: • Stock • Fixed assets (at least quarterly) • Accounts receivable • Accounts payable • Payroll/employee costs		

Ref	Key control activity	Control type (automatic/ manual/ policy)	Control in place (yes/ no/N/A)	Control frequency	Sample size	Is the control appropriately designed to mitigate the risk and has it been implemented as designed?	Testing – has the control operated effectively during the period?	Satisfactory/ Unsatisfactory?	Comments/ recommend-ations for improvement
7.2.5	A process exists to ensure that all control accounts and other trial balance accounts, other than those in 7.2.3 and 7.2.4 above are reconciled at least every six months.								
7.2.6	VAT/Sales Tax, payroll deductions (e.g. PAYE, Social Security, etc.) and pension fund contributions are reviewed by a responsible officer and are reconciled to the general ledger prior to submission.								
8 Employee costs									
8.1 New starters/amendments									
8.1.1	All amendments to payroll standing data are reviewed for validity by an appropriate member of management.								

8.1.2	All new starters/leavers/changes to salaries/terms and conditions and other masterfile amendments are approved by management with the required delegated authority prior to commencement of contract/change to package.				
8.1.3	Appropriate checks are carried out on all new employees and contractors.				
8.2 Payroll and personal expenses					
8.2.1	Payroll is independently reviewed prior to payment.				
8.2.2	All bonus payments, commission payments and advances to employees are documented and appropriately authorised prior to payment.				
8.2.3	All benefits (including relocation packages, childcare allowances, private healthcare and other emoluments) are documented and authorised prior to release.				

Ref	Key control activity	Control type (automatic/manual/policy)	Control in place (yes/no/N/A)	Control frequency	Sample size	Is the control appropriately designed to mitigate the risk and has it been implemented as designed?	Testing – has the control operated effectively during the period?	Satisfactory/Unsatisfactory?	Comments/recommendations for improvement
8.2.4	All personal expense claims have been authorised by the employee's immediate supervisor prior to submission for payment and comply with the firm's policy.								
8.2.5	Issue of company credit cards or electronic payment cards has been approved in writing by the employee's immediate supervisor.								
9 Local Computerised Information Systems (CIS)									
9.1.1	Passwords are maintained and updated in accordance with the firm's IS/IT policy.								

9.1.2	Appropriate controls are in place over the physical security of key local IT hardware resources (e.g. file, print and e-mail servers) including environmental controls.		
9.1.3	Procedures are in place to ensure structured backup of all local key IT systems and databases including end user applications (e.g. spreadsheets).		
9.1.4	Disaster avoidance and recovery procedures are in place and have been tested in accordance with the firm's policy.		